IMAGES OF
Aldershot

IMAGES OF
Aldershot

Stephen Phillips
and Vivienne Owen

First published in Great Britain by
The Breedon Books Publishing Company Limited
Breedon House, 44 Friar Gate, Derby, DE1 1DA.
1998

This paperback edition published in Great Britain in 2015 by DB Publishing, an imprint of JMD Media Ltd

ISBN 978-1-78091-470-1

Printed and bound in the UK by Copytech (UK) Ltd Peterborough

Contents

Introduction

THE aim of this book is not to provide a comprehensive history of Aldershot, but more to capture a feeling of what the town must have been like in years gone by. During the last 30 or 40 years, the face of Aldershot has been dramatically altered, and by no means always for the better. Yet these changes of the 1950s and 1960s are as nothing when compared to the changes that occurred 100 years earlier

Until the arrival of the Army in the 1850s, Aldershot – or 'Aldershott' as it was very often written – was no more than a small village, probably much like dozens of other rural communities in the South of England. A population of 875 in 1851 was transformed into 16,720 ten years later, a level of expansion which was almost certainly unmatched anywhere else in Victorian Britain.

The result of this localised population explosion was a town which had quickly grown up to support the large numbers of troops arriving in the area; it is this Victorian 'New Town' which provides the subject matter of many of the photographs in this book.

The vast majority of these photographs have been taken from the collection held by Aldershot Library. The library itself did not exist until 1954, a full century after the arrival of the Army; consequently, any photographs taken before this date have had to be acquired retrospectively. The late Lt Col Howard Cole, himself a most comprehensive chronicler of Aldershot's history, donated to the library many of the photographs which now appear in this book.

Mr Pat Gale also very kindly lent several postcards of Aldershot, many dating from the turn of the century, and I am greatly indebted to him for his help and generosity in allowing these photographs to appear in these pages.

Many thanks, too, are due to the staff of Aldershot Library for their interest and encouragement; their suggestions and comments have always been of immense help. The various members of the Aldershot Historical and Archae-ological Society have also provided much in the way of support, encouragement, and above all, information.

I hope, therefore, these photographs will be of interest, and will provide a glimpse of the town which earlier generations would have known.

Stephen Phillips
Senior Librarian, Aldershot Library
Hampshire County Library

The Town Centre

Two photographs of Wellington Street taken around the turn of the century, no more than a few years apart, but nonetheless showing several changes. Phillips' moved in on the left (with their clock) in 1901, while the bank building on Victoria Road, visible in the distance has acquired an extra gable.

Two views of Wellington Street in 1958, taken from opposite ends. Judging by the number of people crowded onto the pavements, it is a good thing that this area is now pedestrianised!

A pre-1896 photograph of Wellington Street. The arcade has yet to be built, and the London and County Bank, just visible on the right, has still to receive its 1900 refurbishment.

Wellington Street pictured in about 1905, looking towards High Street. The entrance to the arcade is visible immediately to the left of the bank, and the George Hotel is the building on the left of the photograph.

Wellington Street before the demolition of the shops beyond the Midland Bank. Note the prices in Tesco's window!

Looking up Victoria Road in the 1890s. The Aldershot Institute is in the background, and the large white house in the foreground was demolished to make way for the General Post Office.

Victoria Road in the latter years of the nineteenth century. The twin towers of the Presbyterian Church are clearly visible, but the Post Office is conspicuous by its absence. The residential nature of Victoria Road is still quite obvious.

The Post Office on the corner of Station Road and Victoria Road. It was the town's main Post Office for nearly a century, opening its doors in 1902, before moving to the Wellington Centre in 1996.

The Church of England Soldiers and Sailors Institute in Victoria Road, photographed some time before alterations.were made in 1904, the building having been opened in 1881.

A view of Victoria Road from shortly after the turn of the century. Hunt's the stationers were a long-standing business before closing down in the 1990s.

Victoria Road in 1904, with the Victoria Hotel on the right. The photograph can be dated from the type of cap that the soldiers are wearing.

A 1920s view of Victoria Road with the Church of England Soldiers' and Sailors' Institute prominently shown on the right-hand side.

Looking down Victoria Road in the 1920s. The Victoria Hotel is on the right, while the National Provincial Bank is yet to be built on the corner of Gordon Road.

Looking up Victoria Road in the 1930s towards the Methodist Church in the distance.

Looking up Victoria Road in the 1950s towards the Grosvenor Road Methodist Church. Sadly, the bank, the Soldiers' Institute and beyond that, the Victoria Hotel have all now been demolished.

The corner of Station Road and Victoria Road in the 1950s showing the Post Office, and adjacent to that, shops which have since been demolished.

The corner of Victoria Road and Pickford Street in 1962, showing the Salvation Army Soldiers' Home. All the shops up to the Post Office have since been demolished.

The entrance to the market from Victoria Road. The date of the building – 1935 – is just visible above the arch, and these not unattractive buildings were demolished to make way

Victoria Road taken from just below the junction with Station Road. The Post Office and the Aldershot Institute are on the right-hand corners of Station Road.

Union Street, pictured in about 1903.

Looking down Union Street from Grosvenor Road in the early 1900s.

Union Street in the 1930s. The motor vehicle has not quite vanquished the horse-drawn variety as illustrated by the vehicle outside White's Tea Lounge, on the right.

The top of Union Street looking down the hill towards Wellington Street in 1958.

A busy shopping scene in the late 1950s, looking down Union Street towards Wellington Street.

Two views of High Street, taken from opposite ends. The first is taken with Wellington Street on the right, while the second is looking towards the spot from which the first was taken.

High Street, *c.*1931. The Empire Cinema was opened on 1 August 1930, while the Ritz Cinema had not at this time been built, giving an uninterrupted view of the old Police Station further down the road on the left.

The Empire and Ritz Cinemas in the distance, shortly after the latter was completed in 1937.

Prince's Gardens at the top of High Street in the 1930s. The old Talavera Barracks, since demolished, are in the background.

The Ritz and Empire Cinemas, High Street in 1937. The film showing was *It's a Grand World*, starring Sandy Powell.

A late 1940s view of High Street from the corner of Wellington Street. The Luna Milk Bar is now occupied by Macari's Cafe.

High Street in the years immediately after World War Two. the 'Gentlemen's Convenience, Wash and Brush-Up' has long gone, as have the Police Station and houses, as well as Rangers furniture store on the right-hand side.

An unusual view of the junction of Gun Hill, High Street, Wellington Avenue and Station Road, before the construction of the roundabout.

High Street photographed in 1953, showing hoardings and shops since demolished to make way for the Public Library.

Less than a year later, and the then single-storey library has been built, although it did not open its doors until three weeks after this photograph was taken. The hoarding on the right is celebrating the centenary of the Army coming to Aldershot.

Looking up High Street towards the cinemas, early 1965. The houses on the right are the old police houses, since demolished.

Aldershot Police Station, High Street. The Ritz Cinema is in the background.

W.North grocery shop at 209 High Street, opposite the Recreation Ground.

W.North removals, further along High Street towards the town centre, at the junction with Crimea Road.

High Street. The road leading off to the right is Ordnance Road, while Sebastopol Road leads off to the left.

The Fire Station and Town Hall, both of which were built in 1904. The Municipal Gardens are just visible to the left of the Town Hall.

The Town Hall in Grosvenor Road, undergoing a cleaning of the stonework in August 1950.

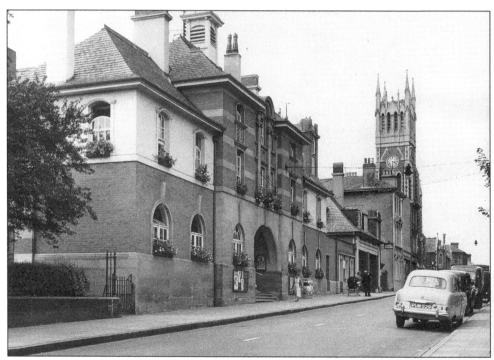

Grosvenor Road in the late 1950s showing (from left to right) the Town Hall, the Fire Station, and further on, the Methodist Church. These buildings are now either being put to use as offices or, as in the case of the Fire Station, has been demolished.

A real temple of convenience situated in Barrack Road. It was demolished in 1959.

The corner of Grosvenor Road and Birchett Road, showing the TGWU District Office, since replaced by more modern accommodation.

Station Road taken round at about the time of World War One. The Palace Cinema is on the left, and the Post Office is on the right.

The Municipal Baths pictured in 1962, in Little Wellington Street. They were opened in September 1961 and were built on the site of the Royal Standard public house.

The Arcade Mews, Little Wellington Street were demolished in the late 1980s to make way for a rebuilt arcade. Before the advent of the motor car it provided stabling for 50 horses; in its latter years it housed only horseless carriages.

The Hippodrome Theatre at the junction of Station Road and Birchett Road in 1922. The Cambridge Military Hospital is just visible in the distance.

A bird's eye view of the junction of Birchett Road and Elms Road, *c.*1960.

A view of Station Road in the 1930s. The railway station is just visible to the top right of the picture while the bus station is just out of the picture to the right.

The east side of Cross Street, looking south towards the somewhat unappealing Riviera Casino.

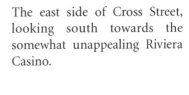

These houses in Frederick Street have now been sympathetically restored, and are in use as offices.

Town Centre Shopping

Gale and Polden in the Grove. This shows the aftermath of a fire in 1918.

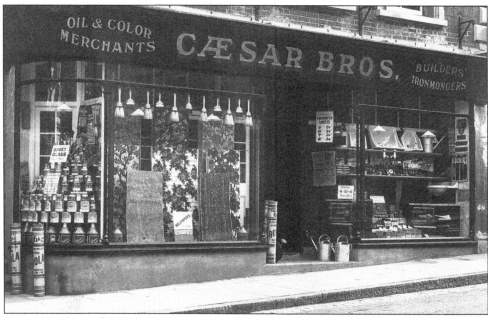

Caesar Brothers of 47 Union Street pictured between the wars. Note the spelling of 'color' above the windows, and some of the prices, too!

Messrs Phillips and Garratt, opticians of 63 High Street.

The Garrison Studio, 109 High Street. This building occupied part of the site of the current Aldershot Library.

A heavily retouched photograph of Bide's florist shop at 97 Victoria Road in 1922.

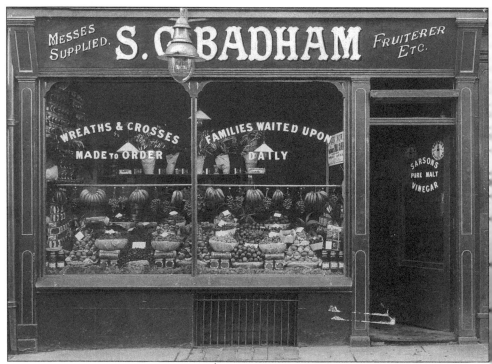

S.G.Badham, greengrocers in Upper Union Street, in 1920.

Opposite ends of the Market Arcade, which linked High Street and Wellington Street.

Time up! F.Phillips the jewellers closed in 1962, having been established in 1856. They moved to these premises on Wellington Street in 1901.

Laslett's clothing and fabric store in Wellington Street, photographed shortly before closing in 1966. The building was ultimately demolished to make way for the Wellington Centre.

The Shamrock Linen Warehouse, Wellington Street, photographed in 1961. The large opening under the word 'Linen' is the entrance to the arcade.

Harlands clothiers, Victoria Road. This shows the other end of the arcade from that shown in the previous photograph.

Boots the Chemists in Wellington Street. This, too, was demolished to make way for the Wellington Centre.

The extensive façade of Thomas White's in Union Street, pictured in 1964.

William May and Co., Ltd. at 175 Victoria Road in 1964.

Harry's Florists and Fruiterers in Victoria Road, situated just below the Post Office, and since demolished.

Wyman and Sons, Victoria Road. This was formerly John Drew (Stationers) Ltd., who had published several directories of the town before World War Two.

The Cheung Fai Chinese restaurant in Station Road, looking towards the round-about on the junction of High Street, Station Road and Wellington Avenue.

A.R.Parsons and Sons of High Street in 1962.

J.C.Rogers, confectioners of 72 High Street, pictured in 1962.

The Fire Brigade pictured in 1954 extinguishing a fire that had broken out in the upper storey of Woolworths, which caused no small damage to their upper floors.

Aldershot Market in full swing, early 1965.

The entrance to Aldershot Market from Victoria Road in 1965.

Watering Holes

The Wheatsheaf in Church Lane East, pictured in about 1910.

The original building of the Heroes of Lucknow in North Lane, pictured in 1892. The licensee, Mr William Spooner, is second from the right. Note the spelling of 'Hero's.

An outing from the Hussar in 1923 or 1924. This public house was in Victoria Road, and closed in the late 1950s. The proprietor, Mr. Biddle, is eighth from the right.

The Victoria Hotel in Victoria Road. The hotel closed immediately after the 1966 Farnborough Air Show. It has since been demolished and a row of shops now occupies the site.

The two-storey bar section of the South Western Hotel has now been replaced by the DSS offices. This photograph dates from 1960.

The Grosvenor Hotel at the junction of Grosvenor Road and Union Street in 1961. Offices now occupy the building.

The Wellington Hotel and the Globe in Wellington Street. Both have since been demolished.

The Duke of York in Weybourne Road in 1952.

Churches

St Michael's Parish Church, from an engraving of about 1856. The church dates from at least the twelfth century, but following the .great increase in population in the mid-nineteenth century, was enlarged from the 1860s onwards.

The church, as seen from Manor Park, c.1911.

A view of the church from Church Lane East in 1929.

A later view, from 1958, taken from near the junction of Church Lane East and Church Hill.

The interior of the Parish Church, taken shortly before World War One.

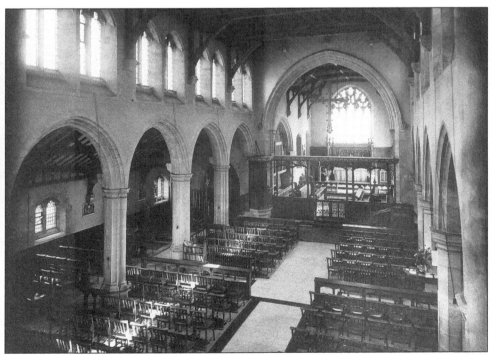

A similar view, but with, amongst other things, the addition of the rood screen and the organ.

A closer look at the rood screen.

The Wesleyan Hall on Queens Road, adjoining the Methodist Church, *c.*1900.

The Methodist Church on Grosvenor Road, photographed in the years before World War One. Now used as offices, it was built in 1874 at a cost of £10,000.

Fifty years later from that of the previous page, and the church still attracts the eye when looking up Victoria Road.

A photograph showing the Soldiers' Home and Methodist Church. Happily, all these buildings survive, although they are now used as either offices or shops.

St Joseph's Roman Catholic Church, Queens Road, *c.*1913. It had been built the previous year, replacing a 'temporary' corrugated iron church on the same site, which had been built in 1872.

The Presbyterian Church and Manse, Victoria Road in about 1900. The church building was begun in 1863, and completed in 1869.

A now impossible view of the side of the church the 1950s, taken from Station Road. The Manse has been demolished, and shops now occupy the site.

The Holy Trinity Church pictured in about 1909, from the Victoria Road side.

The Holy Trinity Church, Albert Road, photographed 20 years apart, in 1938 and 1958 respectively. The foundation stone was laid in 1875, and the church consecrated three years later. The church had strong links with Canadian forces stationed in Aldershot during World War Two.

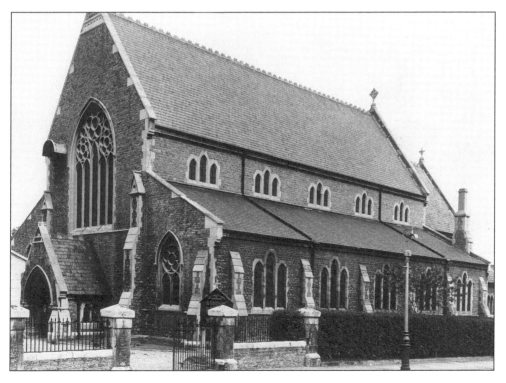

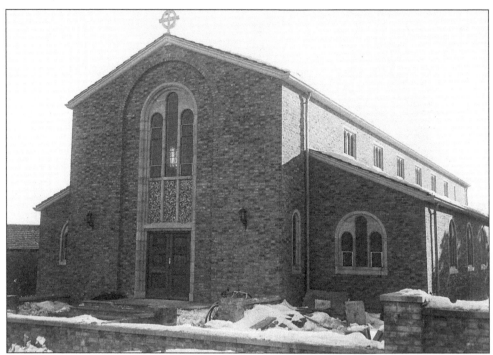

St Mary's Roman Catholic Church, Belle Vue Road in January 1963. The first mass was held on 13 January of that year.

St Saviour's Roman Catholic Church, Church Lane East, which opened in November 1960.

The Rotunda Church at the junction of Albert Road and Victoria Road in about 1910. The church was built in 1876 and belonged to the Primitive Methodists until the Methodist Church united, when it was sold to the Reformed Episcopal Church of England, and renamed Christ Church.

St George's Garrison Church clergy and officers at the consecration ceremony in 1893. The foundation stone had been laid by Queen Victoria the previous year.

A general view of the church in about 1910.

'Church Parade' shortly before World War One, showing Queen's Avenue stretching into the distance.

Two views of All Saints Garrison Church, sometimes known as the 'Red Church', due to the original bright red brickwork. The church was built in 1863 (photographed here in about 1910), and contains many memorials and regimental colours.

The 'Wooden Church' – the Roman Catholic Garrison Church of St Michael and St Sebastien, which stood opposite the Louise Margaret Hospital.

St Andrew's Garrison Church, Queen's Avenue, which occupies the site of the 'Iron Church', one of the first churches in the Camp.

Parks and Gardens

A general view of the town taken from Hungry Hill in the 1930s.

The Manor House, c.1939, before the building of the Heroes' Shrine in the foreground of this photograph. The Manor House was built in 1670 by the Tichborne family who held the manor until about 1750.

A general view of the Heroes' Shrine in Manor Park photographed in the 1950s, from the same position as the previous photograph.

Manor Park from the 1930s, although little changed today. High Street is on the left.

Manor Park again from the 1930s. High Street is on the right in this view.

The rock garden in the Heroes' Shrine is made from stonework from 53 cities bombed during World War Two.

Redan Hill around the turn of the century was evidently a fairly popular place for a stroll or a picnic!

The Municipal Gardens pictured before World War One, looking towards Grosvenor Road, the buildings of which are facing us. The large building just right of centre, is the rear of the Town Hall.

The Municipal Gardens showing the rear of the Town Hall, and to the left of that, the tower of the Methodist Church on Grosvenor Road.

The unveiling of the War Memorial in the Municipal Gardens by Prince Henry, later Duke of Gloucester, on 18 March 1925.

The War Memorial with two captured World War One guns, one German, the other Turkish. They were removed in 1940.

The Prince's Gardens in the 1950s. It was on, or near this spot in 1853 that the first military personnel – a small detachment of Royal Engineers – arrived, and established what was to become the Royal Engineers' Yard. The Borough Council purchased the land from the War Department in 1930. In the background can be seen the gates and buildings of Warburg Barracks.

A small oasis of calm in the gardens at the junction of High Street and Redan Road.

Rowhill Copse occupies approximately 50 acres of land at the corner of Cranmore Lane and Farnborough Road. It functions as a nature reserve, and also provides the source of the River Blackwater which in parts forms the Hampshire-Surrey county boundary.

Rest & Recreation

The Hippodrome immediately prior to demolition in November 1960. Built in 1913, it was for many years the home to variety and music-hall entertainments.

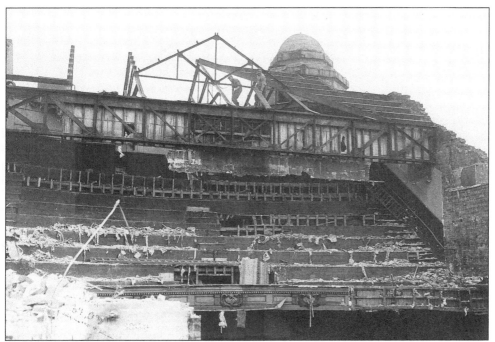

Two views of the Hippodrome during demolition. Note the decorated panelling, which lent a touch of class to the interior of this theatre.

The Theatre Royal. Built in 1891, it was situated on the corner of Birchett Road and Gordon Road, and was demolished in 1959. This photograph was taken in 1945.

The Palace Cinema, Station Road, photographed between the wars. It opened just before World War One, and today houses a night club.

A photograph of the opening of the 'Manor Park Pavilion Picture Theatre', on 27 December 1926.

Two views of the interior of the Pavilion, also from December 1926.

The Pavilion Cinema in 1930, on the occasion of its re-opening showing *Disraeli*. *The Wrecker* would appear to have provided an action-packed follow-up feature!

The Empire Cinema, High Street, photographed in the 1930s. It is now the home of the King's Church.

The Ritz Cinema, High Street in about 1950. The band is that of the 2nd Battalion, the Parachute Regiment.

A general view of the Recreation Ground, taken in the 1950s before the construction of the stand at the near end of the ground.

A slightly later view, looking in the opposite direction, after the construction of the stand.

The next six photographs show various views of the Bathing Pool dating from the 1930s, showing the popularity of the place, as well as the different facilities on offer.

Scraping the bottom in the 1950s!

Highways & Byways

A reminder at the High Street end of Church Hill of the days when Aldershot was a village. The grassy area in the foreground is all that remains of the village green, with the entrance to Manor Park on the right. This area would have been the focal point of the village.

A quiet, almost rural scene, showing the junction between Church Lane East and Church Hill in the early years of the century. Behind the wall on the right is St Michael's Churchyard.

Looking along Grosvenor Road towards the Methodist Church, whose tower is visible in the distance, at about the turn of the century.

An early 1900s view of Cargate Avenue looking towards Church Lane West.

Looking up Eggars Hill in 1951 towards the junction with Grosvenor Road and Church Lane East and West. The house at the junction with Church Lane East has since been demolished.

Ayling Lane in the early years of the century. The old hedgerows on the left can still be clearly seen today.

A rural scene on Farnborough Road before the domination of the motor car. Rowhill Copse is on the right, with Cranmore Lane leading off to the right just beyond it. In the far distance can be seen the spire of the Garrison Church.

The County High School, Highfield Avenue, pictured in the 1930s. The school was opened in 1912, and is pictured here before the building of an extension on the left-hand side.

The school from the north in 1958, showing the newer buildings.

The NAAFI Club, Wellington Avenue was opened in 1948 by the Duke of Gloucester. The building closed in 1971, and was demolished in the 1980s.

Two views of Aldershot Hospital, the foundation stone of which was laid in 1896, it being opened the following year by HRH the Duchess of Connaught and Strathearn. Situated on the corner of Church Lane East and St George's Road, the first photograph was taken soon after its opening, the second nearly 60 years later.

The junction of High Street and Waterloo Road in 1960, showing Manor Cottages. Their site is now occupied by a petrol filling station, while the large building behind and to the left was the Pavilion Cinema.

The Aldershot Gas Works, pictured from Ash Road in 1964, just prior to demolition the following year.

Aldershot Park Mansion in September 1960. The house had been built by Charles Baron in 1842, and was eventually demolished to make way for the development of the bathing pool.

The Farnborough Road Boathouse on the Basingstoke Canal, pictured soon after the beginning of the twentieth century. The spire in the background is that of St George's Church on Queen's Avenue.

The old and the new. The first two photographs show the junctions of North Lane with Alexandra Place and Denmark Street respectively, while the next two photographs show Denmark Street itself, and the new Denmark Square. All photographs date from the 1950s.

Transports of Delight

In the years before World War One, the Army began experimenting with ways of taking to the air, which eventually resulted in the birth of first the Royal Flying Corps, and subsequently, the Royal Air Force. Pictured here are a variety of early aeroplanes, balloons and airships.

Army mono biplane *c.*1912.

Monoplane *c.*1913

Military balloons *c.*1913.

(Paulhan) army aeroplane *c.*1912.

Army airship *Gamma II c.*1910.

Biplane, descending after a good flight in a 30-mile-an-hour wind *c.*1912.

An early bus of about 1913 undergoing maintenance in the workshops.

An Aldershot and District Traction Company charabanc, photographed in about 1926.

A couple of the company's buses in 1930. They had been specially laid on for the Searchlight Tattoo of that year.

Aldershot and District Bus Station, about 1938. The Grove is the road in the background.

The well appointed and spacious Traction Company Hall boasted a sprung floor and is pictured here in the inter-war years.

2-6-0 'N' Class goods engine approaching Aldershot Railway Station in 1965.

The same engine, having just passed under the Five Arch Bridge which carries Church Lane East over the railway.

Royals & Royal Occasions

Two prints from July 1856, showing respectively Queen Victoria inspecting the 'Medal Men', and addressing the troops at 'Aldershott'.

An early print entitled 'Field Day', showing cavalry riding past the Prince and Princess of Wales, the future Edward VII and Queen Alexandra.

King George V taking the salute from a battalion of infantry in 1913, on Queen's Parade.

The Royal Review of June 1913. King George V is accompanied by Sir Douglas Haig, with the buildings along Queen's Avenue visible in the background.

The infantry passing the saluting base on Queen's Avenue on the occasion of the visit of the Shah of Persia on 3 November 1919.

A visit by King George V to the Military Power Station. The station was opened in 1902, decommissioned in 1963, and demolished two years later.

The Royal Party at the Royal Pavilion in the early 1920s. From left to right at the back are Major Reginald Seymour, Hon. Sir Derek Keppel, Lady Ampthill, Lt. Col. Lord Stamfordham and Captain Hon. Alexander Hardinge. Seated are Queen Mary, King George V and Princess Mary.

The planting of oak trees in Manor Park by the Mayor and the Aldershot Chamber of Commerce to mark the Silver Jubilee of King George V in 1935.

Moving into Rushmoor Arena for King George V's Silver Jubilee Review, on 13 July 1935.

The Silver Jubilee Review of the Army by King George V in Rushmoor Arena on 13 July 1935. The Cameronians (Scottish Rifles) are passing the saluting base.

The Mayor of Aldershot, Councillor W.J.North reading the Proclamation of the Accession of King Edward VIII on the Town Hall steps in January 1936.

King George VI and Queen Elizabeth, with Lt. General Wilson during their visit to St Andrew's Garrison Church in 1938.

Sixteen years on from the previous page, top, and a different Mayor, Alderman H.D.Tanner performing the same duties in respect of the accession of Queen Elizabeth II.

A visit inspecting married quarters by King George VI and Queen Elizabeth, the present Queen Mother, in 1938. The figure on the extreme left is the Rt. Hon. Leslie Hore-Belisha, Secretary of State for War.

King Carol and Prince Michael of Rumania in 1939, seen here inspecting a 90cm searchlight and sound locator.

King George VI, accompanied by Sir John Dill, Chief of the Imperial General Staff, visiting the Queen's Own Cameron Highlanders at Ramillies Barracks, in 1939.

A Canadian Scottish Battalion being inspected by King George VI on Queen's Avenue in January 1940.

During the same visit in January 1940, King George VI inspecting troops on Queen's Avenue.

The Mayoral party and official guests at the present Queen's Birthday Parade in 1952. The Mayor is Alderman Tanner.

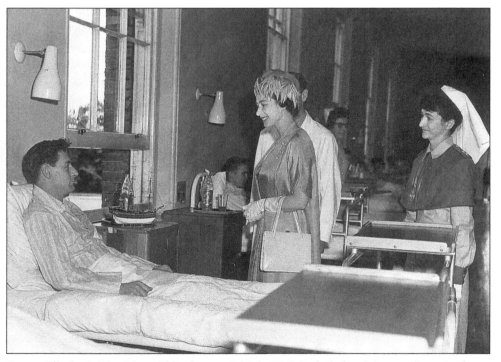

Queen Elizabeth II's visit to Aldershot on 26 July 1963 included a visit to patients in the Cambridge Military Hospital.

People & Parades

The court-martial of Lt. Col. Crawley in 1863 in the large room of the Officers' Club House. He had been charged with causing the death of RSM Lilley in India, by having him arrested, and by the severity of the conditions imposed upon him. It was a cause celebre of the day, and ended in Crawley's acquittal.

Pupils at the West End Infants School, pictured in about 1910. The school celebrated its centenary in 1998.

Mr Cox and his wife at the turn of the century. Mr Cox owned a junk shop on Grosvenor Road.

The chief office of the Aldershot Gas, Water and Lighting Company, pictured in June 1914.

With the Royal Garrison Church of All Saints in the background, the West Surrey Regiment parade at the turn of the century.

Wellington Avenue looking towards the Royal Garrison Church of All Saints in the early years of the century.

The funeral procession of Firemen Perkiss and Hughes passing the Fire Station on Grosvenor Road, 23 January 1911. Their deaths occurred when the ladder with Perkiss at the top fell on Hughes who was killed outright. Perkiss died later in hospital.

The 5th Lancers passing the Wellington Statue at about the turn of the century.

Hospital Hill at the turn of the century, looking towards where it meets the southern end of Queen's Avenue.

An RAMC Church Parade in the early 1900s. The band has come from St George's Church and have turned on to Alisons Road.

As the Royal Engineers leave St George's Church, an unidentified regiment, probably Irish, enter the church. The date is about 1908.

Church parade, Wellington Avenue in about 1908.

A contingent of the Womens' Auxiliary Army Corps marching past King George V and Queen Mary in 1917.

The Headquarters Staff, Aldershot Command, and attached officers after the signing of the armistice to end World War One.

The Aldershot News' 'Old Folks Fund' charity appeal featuring the Black and White Minstrels, in the years between the wars.

The Charter Day Ceremony, 21 June 1922. On the left is General the Rt. Hon. J.B.Seely, Lord Lieutenant of Hampshire. Mr. R.J.Snuggs, Chairman of Aldershot Urban District Council, is about to present the Charter to Mr Arthur H.Smith, Mayor-elect, behind whom is standing Lt. General Sir T.L.N.Morland, GOC Aldershot Command.

The British Legion provide a guard of honour at Aldershot Railway Station on Charter Day for Lord Woolmer, MP for Aldershot, the Mayor-elect of Aldershot, Mr A.H.Smith, and the Lord Lieutenant of Hampshire, General the Rt. Hon. J.B.Seely.

The British Legion contingent march along High Street as part of the Charter Day procession on 21 June 1922.

R.W.Edwards, Mayor of Aldershot from 1929 to 1932.

The Mayoral Procession in Victoria Road in 1929. The Mayor is Councillor R.W.Edwards.

Mayor R.W.Edwards at the Armistice Service at the War Memorial in the Municipal Gardens in 1932.

The Aldershot Gas, Water and District Lighting Company Co-partnership and Hospital Festival, pictured on 28 July 1923.

The Outdoor Staff of the Aldershot Gas, Water and District Lighting Company, pictured in 1929.

Rev. A.E.Chapman was headmaster of Aldershot County School and Vicar of Normandy between the wars.

The staff of the Sport, Tattoo and Show Office in 1937. Given the scale of the Tattoo, it is perhaps surprising that not more staff were required for its organisation.

The Sebastopol Road corner of High Street during the Warship Week procession in February 1942.

'Salute the Soldier' week procession in High Street on 22 July 1944.

The opening of the Harland Hall as Aldershot Scouts and Guides Headquarters in 1944.

The Canadian Womens' Army Corps passing the saluting base on the occasion of the presentation of the Freedom of the Borough to the Canadian Army Overseas, at the Recreation Ground in September 1945.

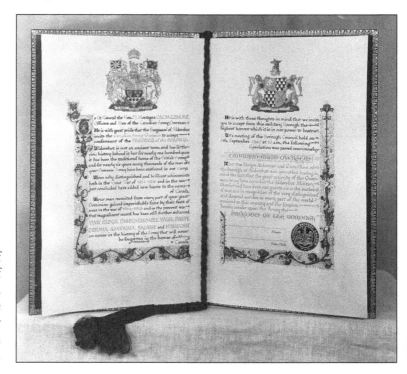

The Scroll of the Freedom of the Borough, presented to the Canadian Army Overseas in 1945.

The march past of the Royal Hampshire Regiment on receiving the Freedom of the Borough in September 1945. The venue is the Recreation Ground.

The band of the Royal Hampshire Regiment leading detachments of seven battalions of the regiment along High Street and on to Ordnance Road in September 1945.

Detachments of seven battalions of the Royal Hampshire Regiment on parade at the Recreation Ground, on 11 September 1945.

Sir Winston Churchill receives the Freedom of the Borough from Councillor G.Roberts, Mayor of Aldershot. The ceremony took place at the Dorchester Hotel, London, on 6 July 1948.

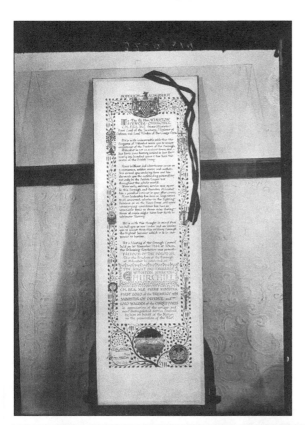

The Scroll of the Freedom of the Borough, granted in 1944, presented to Sir Winston Churchill in 1948.

The Mayoral Sunday Parade in 1950 with the band of the 4th/7th Royal Dragoon Guards in Victoria Road.

The Mayoral Banquet, held on 4 October 1950 in the Traction Company Hall, Halimote Road.

Alderman Lt. Col. H.D.Tanner in Mayoral robes in 1950, accompanied by the Mayoress and Mr D.Llewellyn Griffiths, the Town Clerk and Mr Davis, the mace bearer.

RSM Ronald Brittain, MBE. He was the RSM of the Mons Officer Cadet School from 1942 to 1955.

The opening ceremony of the library on 23 June 1954. Alderman J.Drew is about to open the doors, watched by (left to right) Mrs A.Colvin, Miss R.Benoit, Mr Crosby of Crosby Builders, Mr F.W.Taylor, Borough Surveyor, Alderman W.G.Eddy, Alderman F.Stay, Mr H.Sales, Town Clerk, Mr W.E.French, Borough Librarian, and Rev. T.Dart, Vicar of Aldershot.

In April 1954, 3,000 troops marched through Aldershot to mark the centenary of the arrival of the Army, among them pictured here, the Royal Artillery Band.

The Beating the Bounds Ceremony on Weybourne Road, on 26 June 1954.

A Civic Exhibition was held in Rushmoor Arena in May 1956, attended by the Duke and Duchess of Gloucester.

The Duke of Gloucester chatting to Alderman H.T.Reeves, the Mayor of Aldershot.

A detachment of Spahis ride along Wellington Street in August 1957. They were in Aldershot for the preview of the SSAFA Tattoo at Rushmoor Arena.

Undaunted by the weather, the Old Contemptibles march down Wellington Avenue after the annual service in the Royal Garrison Church on Sunday, 29 August 1958.

Wellington Avenue in 1963. The occasion is the granting of the Freedom of the Borough to the Parachute Regiment.

Military Aldershot

This print dates from April or May 1855. The exact location is unknown, but it could be in the general area now occupied by Talavera Park. The troops are most probably infantry.

A print from the 1850s showing Talavera, Salamanca and Badajos Barracks. The area in the foreground is now occupied by the King's Church and the Prince's Gardens.

An early photograph from about 1870, showing (from right to left) Waterloo Barracks West, Talavera, Salamanca and Badajos Barracks. The Royal Garrison Church is in the background.

'D' Lines, *c.*1893. In the days of the first hutted military camp (1855-56), huts were erected in lines, designated 'A' lines up to 'Z' lines. They were situated south of the Basingstoke Canal and between Farnborough Road and Thornhill Road.

'Z' lines photographed in about 1893.

The South Cavalry Barracks (from 1909 Beaumont Barracks), pictured in 1893.

Hospital Hill looking towards the town, and showing Talavera Barracks on the left.

A view of soldiers at drill at Salamanca Barracks in the early 1900s.

Salamanca Infantry Barracks with accompanying brass band, *c.*1900.

Talavera Barracks in the early 1900s.

The parade ground of Waterloo Barracks West (the Royal Horse Artillery Barracks), looking west towards Talavera, Salamanca and Badajos Barracks, each of which can be identified by the separate glass roofs linking the front and rear barrack blocks.

The south frontages of the Officers' Messes of Salamanca and Badajos Barracks facing Wellington Avenue in about 1894. These buildings were constructed in the period 1856 to 1859 and were demolished between 1960 and 1962.

The imposing façade of the Officers' Mess, Warburg Barracks, probably photographed in the 1930s. The spire of the Royal Garrison Church of All Saints can be seen on the right of the photograph.

The original Headquarters offices of Aldershot District, photographed about 1893. They fulfilled this role from 1856 to 1895, and were situated on the south side of Knollys Road, overlooking Salamanca Barracks.

The Headquarters Offices at the junction of Queen's Avenue and Steeles Road, *c*.1910.

A view of Army Headquarters, Aldershot District in Steeles Road in the early 1900s.

Buller Officers' Mess, Thornhill Road, in the late 1950s.

The South front of the Royal Engineers' Officers' Mess, Gibraltar Barracks between Alisons Road and Steeles Road, pictured in about 1898.

The Officers' Mess, Waterloo Barracks East. Photographed in the mid 1890s, these barracks were built between 1856 and 1859, and were among the first to be demolished in 1959 and 1960 during the rebuilding of the barracks.

The Officers' Mess, Corunna Barracks, built about 1890.

The Command Fire Station on Queen's Avenue in the early 1900s. The building on the left is the Marlborough Lines Infants School.

Pictured about 1897, the Headquarters of the Military Police. Above the door of the smaller building on the left can be seen the words 'PROVT. MAR OFFICE' (Provost Marshal's Office) and was located on Provost Road between Steeles Road and Alisons Road.

The Regimental Institute Block, Oudenarde Barracks, comprising Recreation Room, Reading Room and Lecture Room. Pictured in about 1895, these buildings were situated at the junction of Evelyn Woods Road and Queen's Avenue.

The Army Service Corps Recreation Hall pictured in the last years of the nineteenth century.

The Prince Consort's Library pictured before the building of the Lecture Hall and Reading Room extension in 1911. This photograph is thought to date from about 1890, the library itself having been founded in 1860 by Prince Albert.

The Officers' Club on Farnborough Road, *c.*1890. The site is now occupied by Potter's International Hotel.

Two views of the Officers' Club on Farnborough Road. Originally built in the middle of the nineteenth century, the building as pictured here shows the result of major renovations in the 1930s.

The temporary Public Library in the Sergeants' Mess, Warburg Barracks, October 1962. At the time, the library building in High Street was being converted from a one-storey to a two-storey building. During the severe winter of 1962-63, the building was so difficult to heat, that on more than one occasion a member of library staff was despatched to the derelict wing of the building in order to rip up some floorboards to throw on the wood burning fire!

Another view from a slightly different angle of the Warburg site, now occupied approximately by the Warburg multi-storey car park.

Married quarters in Buller Road, *c.*1897. The spire of St George's Garrison Church in Queen's Avenue can be seen in the background.

Pictured about 1896, married quarters in Buller Road.

The Connaught Hospital, North Camp, photographed in 1916.

The rear view of the Connaught Hospital, photographed at the turn of the century.

The Cambridge Military Hospital was built in 1879 for the then not inconsiderable sum of £45,000. The hospital is named after the Duke of Cambridge, and originally contained 260 beds.

Two 1930s views of the Louise Margaret maternity hospital. It was named after HRH the Duchess of Connaught and Strathearn, who laid the foundation stone on 1 March 1897.

A bird's eye view of Stanhope Lines in the early 1900s, with the Cambridge Military Hospital showing on the skyline.

St Andrew's Soldiers' Home and club, Mandora Road. This was opened in 1915 and demolished in 1966. The badges of Scottish regiments were depicted in stained glass, set into the leaded windows.

The Smith-Dorrien Soldiers' Home on Queen's Avenue, pictured in the early 1900s. The foundation stone was laid by Lt. General Sir Horace Smith-Dorrien on 4 March 1908. In 1914, during the retreat from Mons at the start of World War One, troops under Sir Horace halted the German advance at the Battle of le Cateau, and instilled in the Germans a great respect for the 'contemptible little army', as the Kaiser called the British Expeditionary Force.

The North Camp gymnasium and adjacent swimming baths pictured in the early 1900s.

Two views of the Fox Gymnasium on Queen's Avenue. The first dates from about 1895, while the second would appear to be a few years later.

The interior of the Military Gymnasium, Aldershot, pictured about 1909.

Army Gymnastic instructors themselves being put through their paces in the gymnasium.

The interior of the Army swimming baths, on Queen's Avenue, pictured c.1900.

The Royal Pavilion was built for Queen Victoria in 1855 on a site chosen by Prince Albert. It was demolished in 1963.

The Royal Pavilion has definitely seen better days in this photograph, taken just prior to demolition.

Cavalry training in the Long Valley, *c.*1904.

The Cavalry Jumps in Long Valley, giving an impression of their scale.

A tented encampment at Bourley Bottom, *c.*1910.

Taken from a postcard of around 1909, this shows the 14th King's Hussars returning from Laffans Plain, accompanied by almost another army of small children.

The Military Cemetery, *c.*1910 with the Basingstoke Canal in the background. The cemetery was opened in 1865 and contains the remains of soldiers who have died in Aldershot, as well as those of Samuel Franklin Cody, the first man in this country to have flown an aircraft.

The chapel in the Aldershot Military Cemetery, *c.*1895.

The presentation ceremony at Talavera Barracks on 24 February 1942 of a mobile canteen and kitchen, from the citizens of Guelph, Ontario.

The RAMC Boer War Memorial at the top of Gun Hill. It was unveiled by King Edward VII in 1905.

The memorial on Queen's Avenue to the Officers and Men of the 8th Division in World War One.

Queen's Avenue looking towards North Camp shortly after World War One.

Queen's Avenue looking south from Marlborough Lines in the late 1920s.

Queen's Avenue looking south in the early years of the century. This is a heavily doctored photograph; the group of soldiers and the car have been added to the original, as has the aeroplane, whose propeller appears to have stopped!

Wellington Avenue looking towards the Garrison Church in the 1940s. The buildings on the left occupy land very close to where the Prince's Hall now stands.

Wellington Avenue in the late 1950s, looking towards Farnborough Road. All Saints Church is in the distance, with Salamanca Officers' Mess on the right; this was demolished in 1961.

Hospital Hill in about 1910 looking south, with the Grosvenor Road Methodist Church tower on the skyline.

Hospital Hill, showing Talavera Barracks on the right.

On guard outside the East Cavalry Barrack gates, in about 1908.

Looking down Hospital Hill in about 1906 towards the town.

A view of Hospital Hill from the top, showing the 2nd Division memorial.

Hospital Hill in 1951 looking towards Barrack Road. The buildings on the right of the far side of Wellington Avenue are part of the Warburg Barracks site; those in the centre of the picture were demolished in 1959.

Hospital Hill and the old Talavera Barracks in 1951. The barracks were demolished ten years after this picture was taken.

The statue of the Duke of Wellington, seated on his horse, Copenhagen. The statue was originally erected at Hyde Park Corner in London in 1846, and was subsequently moved to Aldershot in 1885. The sculptor was Matthew Coles Wyatt.

The Time Gun originally stood at the top of Gun Hill until in the late 1870s it was removed to a site opposite the main entrance to the Military Cemetery. It used to be fired twice a day, at one o'clock and at half past nine in the evening, the practice being discontinued during World War One.

A tented encampment in Rushmoor Arena in the early 1900s.

The north front of Beaumont Barracks, *c.*1897. The glass covered verandah was the Officers' Mess and ante-room.

View of Rushmoor Arena, from 1949. In the years before World War Two, the arena had been the venue of the famous Aldershot Tattoo, but by the time this photograph was taken, it had become overgrown and neglected.

The Royal Military Police Riding School, Beaumont Barracks.

On 4 October 1962, Mr James Ramsden, Parliamentary Under Secretary of State for War, unveiled a commemoration stone at Stanhope Lines to mark the rebuilding of the barracks. The stone weighed 70 tons and incorporated crushed rubble from the demolished barracks.

The Officers' Mess, Beaumont Barracks, semi-derelict and awaiting demolition in the early 1970s. The site is now occupied by a housing estate.

From The Air

The junction of High Street and Gun Hill in 1958. The single-storey library is at the bottom of the picture, the Cambridge Military Hospital at the top. The NAAFI Club faces the library across the roundabout.

A closer view of the rear of the Cambridge Military Hospital towards the top of the photograph, with Waterloo Barracks in the foreground.

This photograph shows in the foreground the construction of new Army married quarters. To the right of the two cinemas on High Street is the Warburg car park, next to which stood the temporary library during the addition of an upstairs floor to the High Street building.

This 1962 view of the Recreation Ground also shows the Cambridge Military Hospital, top left.

Taken from above Church Lane East, the Railway Station is on the right, and the road on the extreme left is Grosvenor Road, leading towards the Methodist Church.

The lack of traffic in this town centre view suggests it may have been taken on a Sunday or on a Wednesday, early closing day. The circular construction, centre top, is the old market, and the old police station can be seen where the multi-storey car park on High Street now stands.

A general view of the town a decade and a half later. The Wellington Centre is under construction, right.

ND - #0213 - 270225 - C0 - 234/156/8 - PB - 9781780914701 - Gloss Lamination